I0814809

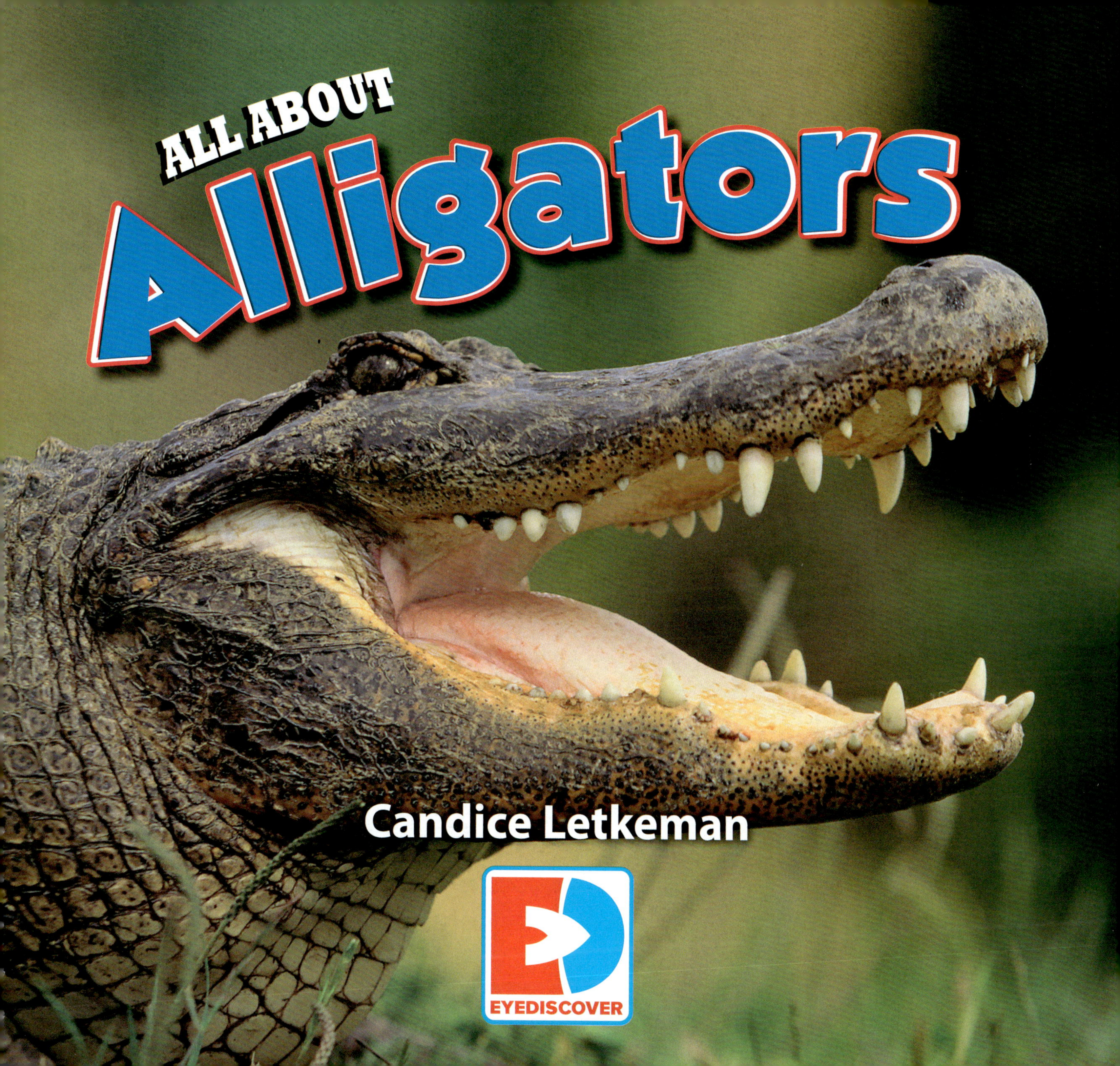
ALL ABOUT
Alligators
Candice Letkeman
EYEDISCOVER

Go to www.eyediscover.com and enter this book's unique code.

BOOK CODE

Y273726

EYEDISCOVER brings you optic readalongs that support active learning.

Published by AV² by Weigl
350 5th Avenue, 59th Floor New York, NY 10118
Website: www.eyediscover.com

Library of Congress Control Number: 2017930770

ISBN 978-1-4896-5641-4 (hardcover)

Printed in the United States of America
in Brainerd, Minnesota
1 2 3 4 5 6 7 8 9 0 21 20 19 18 17

072017
020317

Editor: Katie Gillespie
Designer: Mandy Christiansen

Weigl acknowledges Getty Images, Alamy, iStock, and Dreamstime as the primary image suppliers for this title.

EYEDISCOVER provides enriched content, optimized for tablet use, that supplements and complements this book. EYEDISCOVER books strive to create inspired learning and engage young minds in a total learning experience.

Watch
Video content brings each page to life.

Browse
Thumbnails make navigation simple.

Read
Follow along with text on the screen.

Listen
Hear each page read aloud.

Your EYEDISCOVER Optic Readalongs come alive with...

Audio
Listen to the entire book read aloud.

Video
High resolution videos turn each spread into an optic readalong.

OPTIMIZED FOR

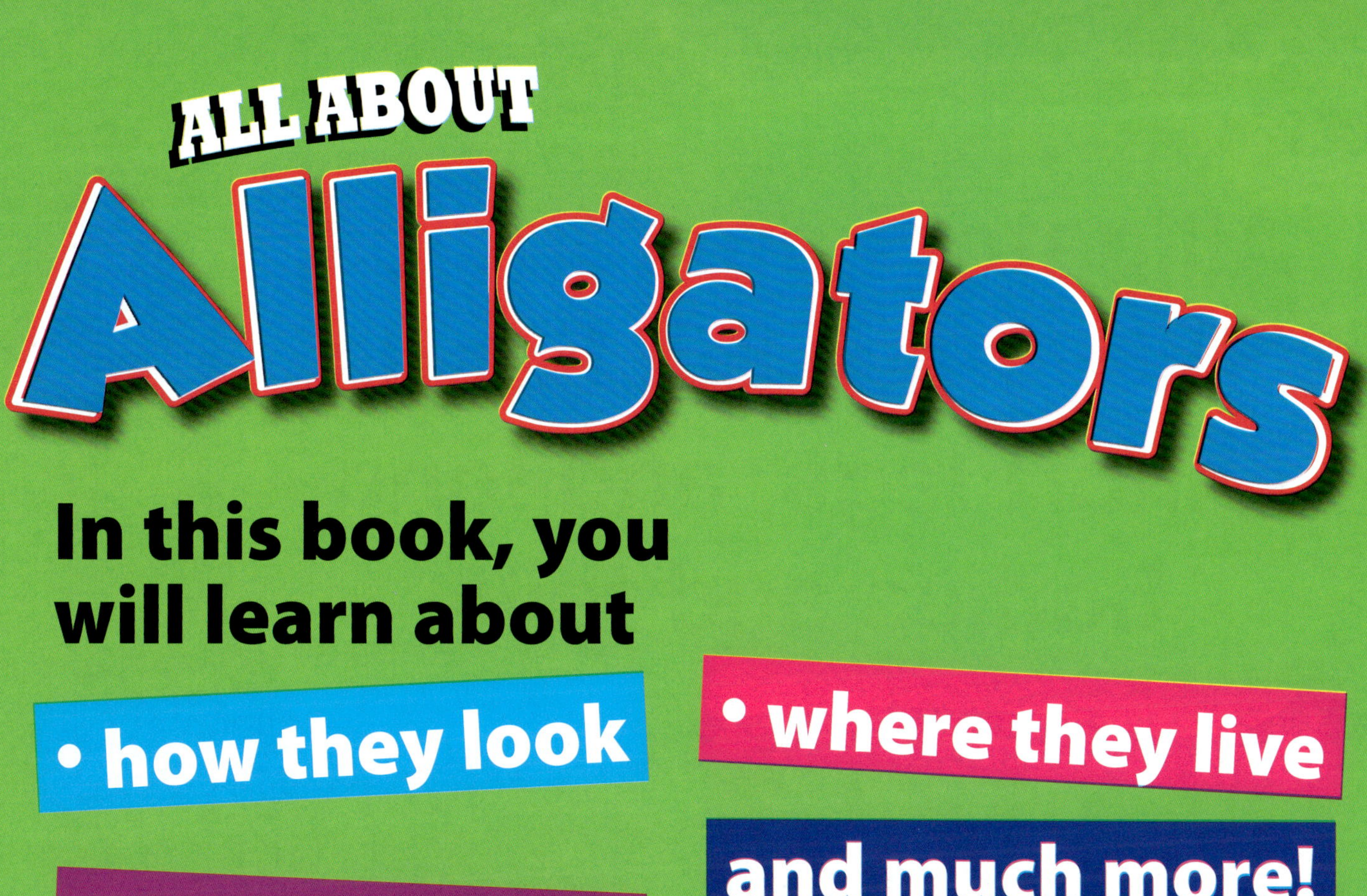

ALL ABOUT Alligators

In this book, you will learn about

- how they look
- what they eat
- where they live

and much more!

Alligators are reptiles. They have big heads, short legs, and long bodies and tails.

Alligators like warm weather. They live in freshwater lakes, rivers, and swamps.

There are only two kinds of alligators. One kind lives in the southern United States. The other kind lives in China.

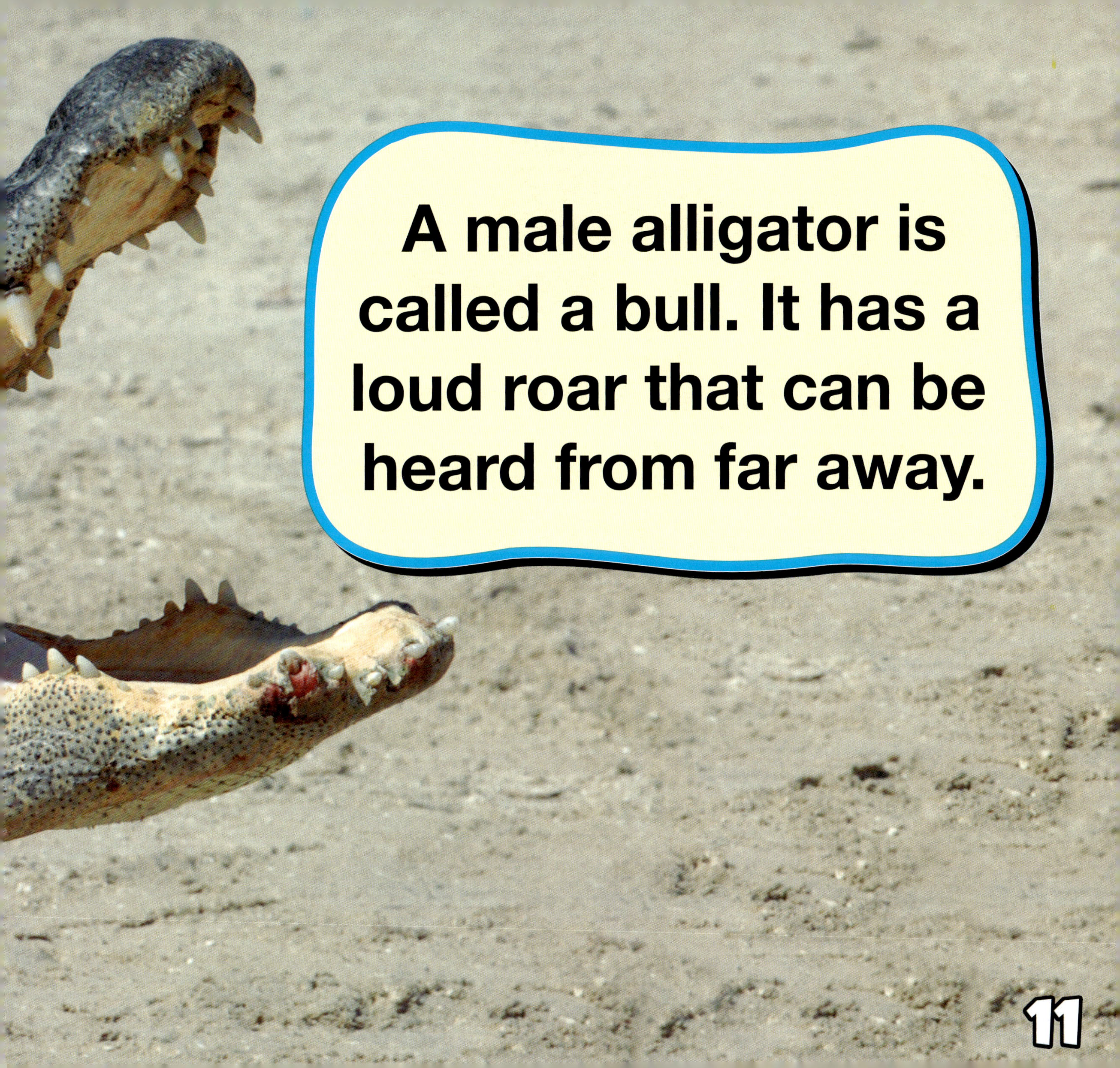

A male alligator is called a bull. It has a loud roar that can be heard from far away.

Baby alligators hatch from eggs. They are very small when they are born.

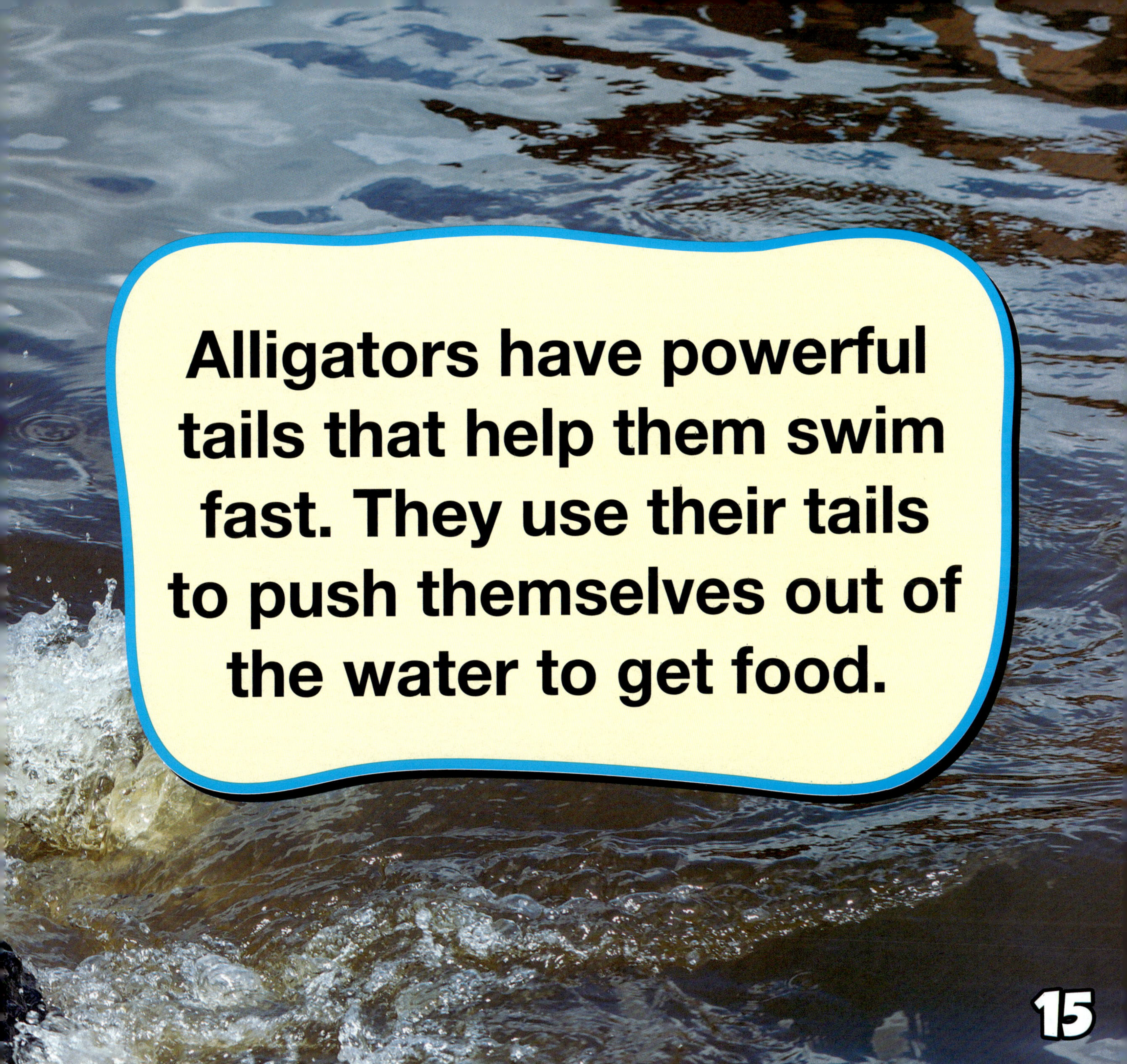

Alligators have powerful tails that help them swim fast. They use their tails to push themselves out of the water to get food.

When an alligator floats at the surface of the water, only its eyes, ears, and nostrils show.

Alligators eat fish, birds, and other small animals.

The number of alligators in nature is getting larger. It is important for people to leave them alone.

Alligators can weigh **up to 1,000 pounds.** (454 kilograms)

Alligators can stay **underwater** for **60 minutes or more.**

Baby **alligators** are **6 to 8** inches long. (15 to 20 centimeters)

Alligators usually lay up to **50 eggs** at a time.

Alligators have **more than 70** teeth. New teeth grow when they wear down. An alligator can have **3,000 teeth** in its lifetime.

Alligators have been around for **more than 180 million years**. Some people call them **living dinosaurs**.

KEY WORDS

Research has shown that as much as 65 percent of all written material published in English is made up of 300 words. These 300 words cannot be taught using pictures or learned by sounding them out. They must be recognized by sight. This book contains 55 common sight words to help young readers improve their reading fluency and comprehension. This book also teaches young readers several important content words, such as proper nouns. These words are paired with pictures to aid in learning and improve understanding.

Page	Sight Words First Appearance
4	and, are, big, have, heads, long, they
7	in, like, live, rivers
8	kinds, of, one, only, other, the, there, two
11	a, away, be, can, far, from, has, heard, is, it, that
12	small, very, when
15	food, get, help, out, their, them, to, use, water
17	an, at, eyes, its, show
19	animals, eat
20	for, important, larger, leave, number, people

Page	Content Words First Appearance
4	alligators, bodies, legs, reptiles, tails
7	lakes, swamps, weather
8	China, United States
11	bull, roar
12	eggs
15	themselves
17	ears, nostrils, surface
19	birds, fish
20	nature

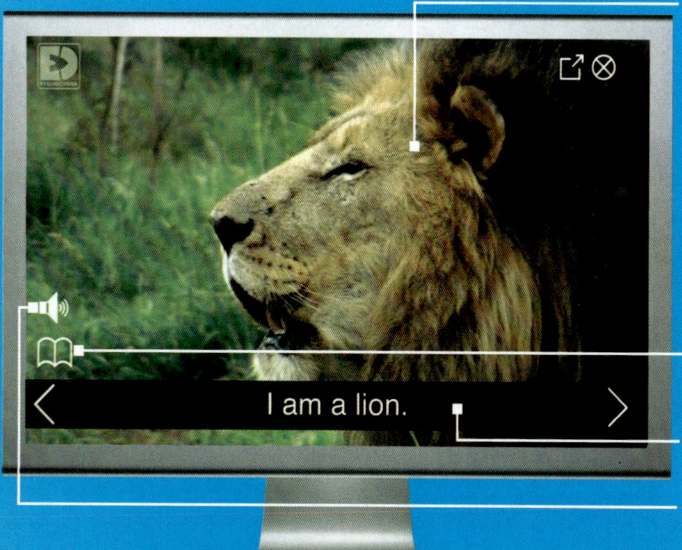

Watch
Video content brings each page to life.

Browse
Thumbnails make navigation simple.

Read
Follow along with text on the screen.

Listen
Hear each page read aloud.

Go to www.eyediscover.com and enter this book's unique code.

BOOK CODE

Y273726